Amish Friendship
Sampler

Oxmoor
House®

AMISH FRIENDSHIP SAMPLER
From the *Quilts Made Easy* ® series
©1997 by Oxmoor House, Inc.

Book Division of Southern Progress Corporation
P.O. Box 2463, Birmingham, AL 35201

Published by Oxmoor House, Inc., and
Leisure Arts, Inc.

Library of Congress Catalog Number: 97-67088
ISBN: 0-8487-1295-1

Manufactured in the United States of America
Second Printing 2000
Quilts Made Easy ® is a federally registered
trademark of Oxmoor House, Inc.

Editor-in-Chief: Nancy Fitzpatrick Wyatt
Editorial Director, Special Interest Publications:
   Ann H. Harvey
Senior Crafts Editor: Susan Ramey Cleveland
Senior Editor, Editorial Services: Olivia Kindig Wells
Art Director: James Boone

AMISH FRIENDSHIP SAMPLER
Editor: Janica Lynn York
Editorial Assistant: Allison D. Ingram
Copy Editor: Karla Higgs
Senior Designer: Larry Hunter
Designer: Lisa Richter
Illustrator: Kelly Davis
Publishing Systems Administrator: Rick Tucker
Senior Photographer: John O'Hagan
Photographer: Keith Harrelson
Photo Stylist: Katie Stoddard
Production and Distribution Director: Phillip Lee
Associate Production Manager: Vanessa C. Richardson

We're Here for You!
We at Oxmoor House are dedicated to serving you
with reliable information that expands your imagi-
nation and enriches your life. We welcome your
comments and suggestions. Please write us at:
Oxmoor House, Inc.
Editor, Amish Friendship Sampler
2100 Lakeshore Drive
Birmingham, AL 35209

To order additional publications, please call
1-205-877-6560.

Contents

Dear Quilting Friends,

The Split Bar set that Susan Stein used in her colorful sampler is most often associated with Pennsylvanian Amish quilts.

Just for fun, and to make her quilt more interesting, Susan added a few intentional color "mistakes" when making the Pinwheel and Flying Geese blocks. See if you can spot the blocks with the mistakes. Following the custom of friendship quilts, each of the sampler blocks carries the signature of a different friend.

These 14 traditional blocks are all easy to piece. So sort out your solids and make your own version. If you prefer a different color scheme, perhaps incorporating prints, use the blank diagrams of each block to help plan your quilt.

Happy Stitching,

Susan Ramey Cleveland

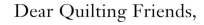

WORKSHOP

Selecting Fabrics

The best fabric for quilts is 100% cotton. Yardage requirements are based on 44"-wide fabric and allow for shrinkage. All fabrics, including backing, should be machine-washed, dried, and pressed before cutting. Use warm water and detergent but not fabric softener.

Necessary Notions

- Scissors
- Rotary cutter and mat
- Acrylic rulers
- Template plastic
- Pencils for marking cutting lines
- Sewing needles
- Sewing thread
- Sewing machine
- Seam ripper
- Pins
- Iron and ironing board
- Quilting needles
- Thimble
- Hand quilting thread
- Machine quilting thread

Making Templates

A template is a duplication of a printed pattern, made from a sturdy material, which is traced onto fabric. Many regular shapes such as squares and triangles can be marked directly on the fabric with a ruler, but you need templates for other shapes. Some quiltmakers use templates for all shapes.

You can trace patterns directly onto template plastic. Or make a template by tracing a pattern onto graph paper and gluing the paper to posterboard or sandpaper. (Sandpaper will not slip on fabric.)

When a large pattern is given in two pieces, make one template for the complete piece.

Cut out the template on the marked line. It is important that a template be traced, marked, and cut accurately. If desired, punch out corner dots with a ⅛"-diameter hole punch **(Diagram 1)**.

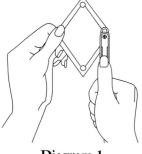

Diagram 1

Mark each template with its letter and grain line. Verify the template's accuracy, placing it over the printed pattern. Any discrepancy, however small, is multiplied many times as the quilt is assembled. Another way to check templates' accuracy is to make a test block before cutting more pieces.

Tracing Templates on Fabric

For hand piecing, templates should be cut to the finished size of the piece so seam lines can be marked on the fabric. Avoiding the selvage, place the template *facedown* on the *wrong* side of the fabric, aligning the template grain line with the straight grain. Hold the template firmly and trace around it. Repeat as needed, leaving ½" between tracings **(Diagram 2)**.

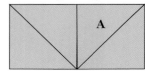

Diagram 2

For machine piecing, templates should include seam allowances. These templates are used in the same manner as for hand piecing, but you can mark the fabric using common lines for efficient cutting **(Diagram 3)**. Mark corners on fabric through holes in the template.

Diagram 3

For hand or machine piecing, use window templates to enhance accuracy by drawing and cutting out both cutting and sewing lines. The guidance of a drawn seam line is very useful for sewing set-in seams, when pivoting at a precise point is critical. Used on the right side of the fabric, window templates help you cut specific motifs with accuracy **(Diagram 4)**.

Diagram 4

For hand appliqué, templates should be made the finished size. Place templates *faceup* on the *right* side of the fabric. Position tracings at least ½" apart **(Diagram 5)**. Add a ¼" seam allowance around pieces when cutting.

Diagram 5

Cutting

Grain Lines

Woven threads form the fabric's grain. Lengthwise grain, parallel to the selvages, has the least stretch; crosswise grain has a little more give.

Long strips such as borders should be cut lengthwise whenever possible and cut first to ensure that you have the necessary length. Usually, other pieces can be cut aligned with either grain.

Bias is the 45° diagonal line between the two grain directions. Bias has the most stretch and is used for curving strips such as flower stems. Bias is often preferred for binding.

Never use the selvage (finished edge). Selvage does not react to washing, drying, and pressing like the rest of the fabric and may pucker when the finished quilt is laundered.

Rotary Cutting

A rotary cutter, used with a protective mat and a ruler, takes getting used to but is very efficient for cutting strips, squares, and triangles. A rotary cutter is fast because you can measure and cut multiple layers with a single stroke, without templates or marking. It is also more accurate than cutting with scissors because fabrics remain flat and do not move during cutting.

Because the blade is very sharp, be sure to get a rotary cutter with a safety guard. Keep the guard in the safe position at all times, except when making a cut. *Always keep the cutter out of the reach of children.*

Use the cutter with a self-healing mat. A good mat for cutting strips is at least 23" wide.

1. Squaring the fabric is the first step in accurate cutting. Fold the fabric with selvages aligned. With the yardage to your right, align a small square ruler with the fold near the cut edge. Place a long ruler against the left side of the square (**Diagram 6**). Keeping the long ruler in place, remove the square. Hold the ruler in place with your left hand as you cut, rolling the cutter *away from you* along the ruler's edge with a steady motion. You can move your left hand along the ruler as you cut, but do not change the position of the ruler. *Keep your fingers away from the ruler's edge when cutting.*

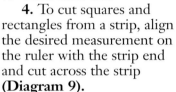
Diagram 6

2. Open the fabric. If the cut was not accurately perpendicular to the fold, the edge will be V-shaped instead of straight (**Diagram 7**). Correct the cut if necessary.

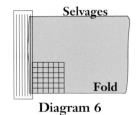
Diagram 7

3. With a transparent ruler, you can measure and cut at the same time. Fold the fabric in half again, aligning the selvages with the fold, making four layers that line up perfectly along the cut edge. Project instructions designate the strip width needed. Position the ruler to measure the correct distance from the edge (**Diagram 8**) and cut. The blade will easily cut through all four layers. Check the strip to be sure the cut is straight. The strip length is the width of the fabric, approximately 43" to 44". Using the ruler again, trim selvages, cutting about ⅜" from each end.

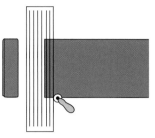
Diagram 8

4. To cut squares and rectangles from a strip, align the desired measurement on the ruler with the strip end and cut across the strip (**Diagram 9**).

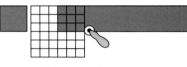
Diagram 9

5. Cut triangles from squares or rectangles. Cutting instructions often direct you to cut a square in half or in quarters diagonally to make right triangles, and this technique can apply to rectangles, too (**Diagram 10**). The outside edges of the square or rectangle are on the straight of the grain, so triangle sides cut on the diagonal are bias.

Diagram 10

6. Some projects in this book use a time-saving technique called strip piecing. With this method, strips are joined to make a pieced band. Cut across the seams of this band to cut preassembled units (**Diagram 11**).

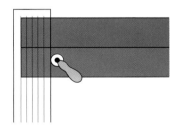
Diagram 11

Machine Piecing

Your sewing machine does not have to be a new, computerized model. A good straight stitch is all that's necessary, but it may be helpful to have a nice satin stitch for appliqué. Clean and oil your machine regularly, use good-quality thread, and replace needles frequently.

1. Patches for machine piecing are cut with the seam allowance included, but the sewing line is not usually marked. Therefore, a way to make a consistent ¼" seam is essential. Some presser feet have a right toe that is ¼" from the needle. Other machines have an adjustable needle that can be set for a ¼" seam. If your machine has neither feature, experiment to find how the fabric must be placed to make a ¼" seam. Mark this position on the presser foot or throat plate.

2. Use a stitch length that makes a strong seam but is not too difficult to remove with a seam ripper. The best setting is usually 10 to 12 stitches per inch.

3. Pin only when really necessary. If a straight seam is less than 4" and does not have to match an adjoining seam, pinning is not necessary.

4. When intersecting seams must align **(Diagram 12)**, match the units with right sides facing and push a pin through both seams at the seam line. Turn the pinned unit to the right side to check the alignment; then pin securely. As you sew, remove each pin just before the needle reaches it.

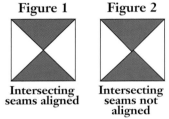

Figure 1

Figure 2

Intersecting seams aligned

Intersecting seams not aligned

Diagram 12

5. Block assembly diagrams are used throughout this book to show how pieces should be joined. Make small units first; then join them in rows and continue joining rows to finish the block **(Diagram 13)**. Blocks are joined in the same manner to complete the quilt top.

Diagram 13

6. Chain piecing saves time. Stack pieces to be sewn in pairs, with right sides facing. Join the first pair as usual. At the end of the seam, do not backstitch, cut the thread, or lift the presser foot. Just feed in the next pair of pieces—the machine will make a few stitches between pieces before the needle strikes the second piece of fabric. Continue sewing in this way until all pairs are joined. Stack the chain of pieces until you are ready to clip them apart **(Diagram 14)**.

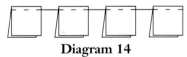

Diagram 14

7. Most seams are sewn straight across, from raw edge to raw edge. Since they will be crossed by other seams, they do not require backstitching to secure them.

8. When piecing diamonds or other angled seams, you may need to make set-in seams. For these, always mark the corner dots (shown on the patterns) on the fabric pieces. Stitch one side, starting at the outside edge and being careful not to sew beyond the dot into the seam allowance **(Diagram 15, Figure A)**. Backstitch. Align the other side of the piece as needed, with right sides facing. Sew from the dot to the outside edge **(Figure B)**.

9. Sewing curved seams requires extra care. First, mark the centers of both the convex (outward) and concave (inward) curves **(Diagram 16)**. Staystitch just inside the seam allowance of both pieces. Clip the concave piece to the stitching **(Figure A)**. With right sides facing and raw edges aligned, pin the two patches together at the center **(Figure B)** and at the left edge **(Figure C)**. Sew from edge to center, stopping frequently to check that the raw edges are aligned. Stop at the center with the needle down. Raise the presser foot and pin the pieces together from the center to the right edge. Lower the foot and continue to sew. Press seam allowances toward the concave curve **(Figure D)**.

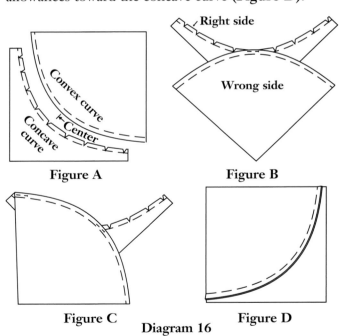

Right side

Wrong side

Convex curve

Concave curve

Center

Figure A

Figure B

Figure C

Diagram 16

Figure D

Hand Piecing

Make a running stitch of 8 to 10 stitches per inch along the marked seam line on the wrong side of the fabric. Don't pull the fabric as you sew; let the pieces lie relaxed in your hand. Sew from seam line to seam line, not from edge to edge as in machine piecing.

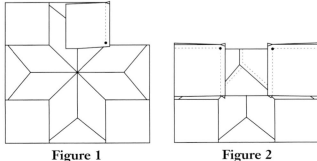

Figure 1

Figure 2

Diagram 15

When ending a line of stitching, backstitch over the last stitch and make a loop knot **(Diagram 17)**.

Match seams and points accurately, pinning patches together before piecing. Align match points as described in Step 4 under Machine Piecing.

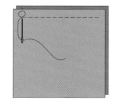

Diagram 17

When joining units where several seams meet, do not sew over seam allowances; sew *through* them at the match point **(Diagram 18)**. When four or more seams meet, press the seam allowances in the same direction to reduce bulk **(Diagram 19)**.

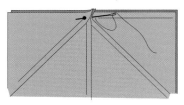

Diagram 18

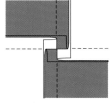

Diagram 19

Pressing

Careful pressing is necessary for precise piecing. Press each seam as you go. Sliding the iron back and forth may push the seam out of shape. Use an up-and-down motion, lifting the iron from spot to spot. Press the seam flat on the wrong side. Open the piece and, on the right side, press both seam allowances to one side (usually toward the darker fabric). Pressing the seam open leaves tiny gaps through which batting may beard.

Appliqué

Traditional Hand Appliqué

Hand appliqué requires that you turn under a seam allowance around the shape to prevent frayed edges.

1. Trace around the template on the right side of the fabric. This line indicates where to turn the seam allowance. Cut each piece approximately ¼" outside the line.

2. For simple shapes, turn the edges by pressing the seam allowance to the back; complex shapes may require basting the seam allowance. Sharp points and strong curves are best appliquéd with freezer paper. Clip curves to make a smooth edge. With practice, you can work without pressing seam allowances, turning edges under with the needle as you sew.

3. Do not turn under any seam allowance that will be covered by another appliqué piece.

4. To stitch, use one strand of cotton-wrapped polyester sewing thread in a color that matches the appliqué. Use a slipstitch, but keep the stitch very small on the surface. Working from right to left (or left to right if you're left-handed), pull the needle through the

base fabric and catch only a few threads on the folded edge of the appliqué. Reinsert the needle into the base fabric, under the top thread on the appliqué edge to keep the thread from tangling **(Diagram 20)**.

5. An alternative to slipstitching is to work a decorative buttonhole stitch around each figure **(Diagram 21)**.

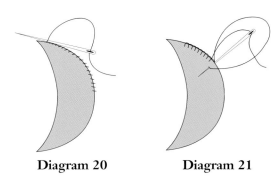

Diagram 20   **Diagram 21**

Freezer Paper Hand Appliqué

Supermarket freezer paper saves time because it eliminates the need for basting seam allowances.

1. Trace the template onto the *dull* side of the freezer paper and cut the paper on the marked line. *Note:* If a design is not symmetrical, turn the template over and trace a mirror image so the fabric piece won't be reversed when you cut it out.

2. Pin the freezer-paper shape, with its *shiny side* up, to the *wrong side* of the fabric. Following the paper shape and adding a scant ¼" seam allowance, cut out the fabric piece. Do not remove pins.

3. Using just the tip of a dry iron, press the seam allowance to the shiny side of the paper. Be careful not to touch the freezer paper with the iron.

4. Appliqué the piece to the background as in traditional appliqué. Trim the fabric from behind the shape, leaving ¼" seam allowances. Separate the freezer paper from the fabric with your fingernail and pull gently to remove it. If you prefer not to trim the background fabric, pull out the freezer paper before you complete stitching.

5. Sharp points require special attention. Turn the point down and press it **(Diagram 22, Figure A)**. Fold the seam allowance on one side over the point and press **(Figure B)**; then fold the other seam allowance over the point and press **(Figure C)**.

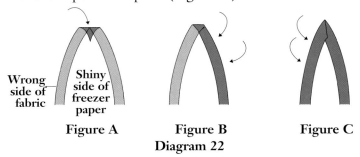

Wrong side of fabric

Shiny side of freezer paper

Figure A   **Figure B**   **Figure C**

Diagram 22

6. When pressing curved edges, clip sharp inward curves **(Diagram 23).** If the shape doesn't curve smoothly, separate the paper from the fabric with your fingernail and try again.

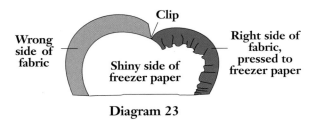

Diagram 23

7. Remove the pins when all seam allowances have been pressed to the freezer paper. Position the prepared appliqué right side up on the background fabric. Press to adhere it to the background fabric.

Machine Appliqué

A machine-sewn satin stitch makes a neat edging. For machine appliqué, cut appliqué pieces without adding seam allowances.

Using fusible web to adhere pieces to the background adds a stiff extra layer to the appliqué and is not appropriate for some quilts. It is best used on small pieces, difficult fabrics, or for wall hangings and accessories in which added stiffness is acceptable. The web prevents fraying and shifting during appliqué.

Place tear-away stabilizer under the background fabric behind the appliqué. Machine-stitch the appliqué edges with a satin stitch or close-spaced zigzag **(Diagram 24).** Test the stitch length and width on a sample first. Use an open-toed presser foot. Remove the stabilizer when appliqué is complete.

Diagram 24

Measuring Borders

Because seams may vary and fabrics may stretch a bit, opposite sides of your assembled quilt top may not be the same measurement. You can (and should) correct this when you add borders.

Measure the length of each side of the quilt. Trim the side border strips to match the *shorter* of the two sides. Join borders to the quilt as described below, easing the longer side of the quilt to fit the border. Join borders to the top and bottom edges in the same manner.

Straight Borders

Side borders are usually added first **(Diagram 25).** With right sides facing and raw edges aligned, pin the center of one border strip to the center of one side of

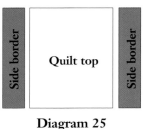

Diagram 25

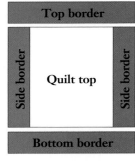

Diagram 26

the quilt top. Pin the border to the quilt at each end and then pin along the side as desired. Machine-stitch with the border strip on top. Press the seam allowance toward the border. Trim excess border fabric at each end. In the same manner, add the border to the opposite side and then the top and bottom borders **(Diagram 26).**

Mitered Borders

1. Measure your quilt sides. Trim the side border strips to fit the shorter side *plus* the width of the border *plus* 2".

2. Center the measurement of the shorter side on one border strip, placing a pin at each end and at the center of the measurement.

3. With right sides facing and raw edges aligned, match the pins on the border strip to the center and corners of the longer side of the quilt. (Border fabric will extend beyond the corners.)

4. Start machine-stitching at the top pin, backstitching to lock the stitches. Continue to sew, easing the quilt between pins. Stop at the last pin and backstitch. Join remaining borders in the same manner. Press seam allowances toward borders.

5. With right sides facing, fold the quilt diagonally, aligning the raw edges of adjacent borders. Pin securely **(Diagram 27).**

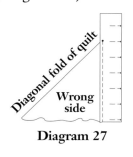

Diagram 27

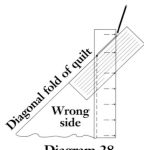

Diagram 28

6. Align a yardstick or quilter's ruler along the diagonal fold **(Diagram 28).** Holding the ruler firmly, mark a line from the end of the border seam to the raw edge.

7. Start machine-stitching at the beginning of the marked line, backstitch, and then stitch on the line out to the raw edge.

8. Unfold the quilt to be sure that the corner lies flat. Correct the stitching if necessary. Trim the seam allowance to ¼".

9. Miter the remaining corners in the same manner. Press the corner seams open.

Quilting Without Marking

Some quilts can be quilted in-the-ditch (right along the seam line), outline-quilted (¼" from the seam line), or echo-quilted (lines of quilting rippling outward from the design like waves on a pond). These methods can be used without any marking at all. If you are machine quilting, simply use the edge of your presser foot and the seam line as a guide. If you are hand quilting, by the time you have pieced a quilt top, your eye will be practiced enough for you to produce straight, even quilting without the guidance of marked lines.

Marking Quilting Designs

Many quilters like to mark the entire top at one time, a practice that requires long-lasting markings. The most common tool for this purpose is a sharp **pencil.** However, most pencils are made with an oil-based graphite lead, which often will not wash out completely. Look for a high-quality artist's pencil marked "2H" or higher (the higher the number, the harder the lead, and the lighter the line it will make). Sharpen the pencil frequently to keep the line on the fabric thin and light. Or try a mechanical pencil with a 0.5-mm lead. It will maintain a fine line without sharpening.

While you are in the art supply store, get a **white plastic eraser** (brand name Magic Rub). This eraser, used by professional drafters and artists, will cleanly remove the carbon smudges left by pencil lead without fraying the fabric or leaving eraser crumbs.

Water- and **air-soluble marking pens** are convenient, but controversial, marking tools. Some quilters have found that the marks reappear, often up to several years later, while others have no problems with them.

Be sure to test these pens on each fabric you plan to mark and *follow package directions exactly.* Because the inks can be permanently set by heat, be very careful with a marked quilt. Do not leave it in your car on a hot day and never touch it with an iron until the marks have been removed. Plan to complete the quilting within a year after marking it with a water-soluble pen.

Air-soluble pens are best for marking small sections at a time. The marks disappear within 24 to 48 hours, but the ink remains in the fabric until it is washed. After the quilt is completed and before it is used, rinse it twice in clear, cool water, using no soap, detergent, or bleach. Let the quilt air-dry.

For dark fabrics, the cleanest marker you can use is a thin sliver of pure, white **soap.** Choose a soap that contains no creams, deodorants, dyes, or perfumes; these added ingredients may leave a residue on the fabric.

Other marking tools include **colored pencils** made specifically for marking fabric and **tailor's chalk** (available in powdered, stick, and traditional cake form). When using chalk, mark small sections of the quilt at a time because the chalk rubs off easily.

Quilting Stencils

Quilting patterns can be purchased as precut stencils. Simply lay these on your quilt top and mark the design through the cutout areas.

To make your own stencil of a printed quilting pattern, such as the one below, use a permanent marker to trace the design onto a blank sheet of template plastic. Then use a craft knife to cut out the design.

Quilting Stencil Pattern

Making a Quilt Backing

Some fabric and quilt shops sell 90" and 108" widths of 100% cotton fabric that are very practical for quilt backing. However, the instructions in this book always give backing yardage based on 44"-wide fabric.

When using 44"-wide fabric, all quilts wider than 41" will require a pieced backing. For quilts 41" to 80" wide, you will need an amount of fabric equal to two times the desired *length* of the unfinished backing. (The unfinished backing should be at least 3" larger on all sides than the quilt top.)

The simplest method of making a backing is to cut the fabric in half widthwise **(Diagram 29),** and then sew the two panels together lengthwise. This results in a backing with a vertical center seam. Press the seam allowances to one side.

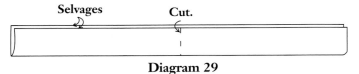

Diagram 29

Another method of seaming the backing results in two vertical seams and a center panel of fabric. This method is often preferred by quilt show judges. Begin by cutting the fabric in half widthwise. Open the two lengths and stack them, with right sides facing and selvages aligned. Stitch along *both* selvage edges to create a tube of fabric **(Diagram 30).** Cut down the center of the top layer of fabric only and open the fabric flat **(Diagram 31).** Press seam allowances to one side.

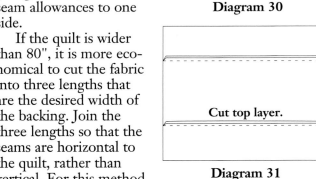

Diagram 30

Diagram 31

If the quilt is wider than 80", it is more economical to cut the fabric into three lengths that are the desired width of the backing. Join the three lengths so that the seams are horizontal to the quilt, rather than vertical. For this method, you'll need an amount of fabric equal to three times the *width* of the unfinished backing.

Fabric requirements in this book reflect the most economical method of seaming the backing fabric.

Layering and Basting

After the quilt top and backing are made, the next steps are layering and basting in preparation for quilting.

Prepare a large working surface to spread out the quilt—a large table, two tables pushed together, or the floor. Place the backing on the working surface wrong side up. Unfold the batting and place it on top of the backing, smoothing away any wrinkles or lumps.

Lay the quilt top wrong side down on top of the batting and backing. Make sure the edges of the backing and quilt top are parallel.

Knot a long strand of sewing thread and use a long (darning) needle for basting. Begin basting in the center of the quilt and baste out toward the edges. The basting stitches should cover an ample amount of the quilt so that the layers do not shift during quilting.

Machine quilters use nickel-plated safety pins for basting so there will be no basting threads to get caught on the presser foot. Safety pins, spaced approximately 4" apart, can be used by hand quilters, too.

Hand Quilting

Hand-quilted stitches should be evenly spaced, with the spaces between stitches about the same length as the stitches themselves. The *number* of stitches per inch is less important than the *uniformity* of the stitching. Don't worry if you take only five or six stitches per inch; just be consistent throughout the project.

Machine Quilting

For machine quilting, the backing and batting should be 3" larger all around than the quilt top, because the quilting process pushes the quilt top fabric outward. After quilting, trim the backing and batting to the same size as the quilt top.

Thread your bobbin with good-quality sewing thread (not quilting thread) in a color to match the backing. Use a top thread color to match the quilt top or use invisible nylon thread.

An even-feed or walking foot will feed all the quilt's layers through the machine at the same speed. It is possible to machine-quilt without this foot (by experimenting with tension and presser foot pressure), but it will be much easier *with* it. If you do not have this foot, get one from your sewing machine dealer.

Straight-Grain Binding

1. Mark the fabric in horizontal lines the width of the binding (**Diagram 32**).

A	↕ width of binding	
B		A
C		B
D		C
E		D
F		E
		F

Diagram 32

2. With right sides facing, fold the fabric in half, offsetting drawn lines by matching letters and raw edges (**Diagram 33**). Stitch a ¼" seam.

3. Cut the binding in a continuous strip, starting with one end and following the marked lines around the tube. Press the strip in half lengthwise.

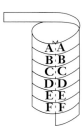

Diagram 33

Continuous Bias Binding

This technique can be used to make continuous bias for appliqué as well as for binding.

1. Cut a square of fabric in half diagonally to form two triangles. With right sides facing, join the triangles (**Diagram 34**). Press the seam allowance open.

Diagram 34

2. Mark parallel lines the desired width of the binding (**Diagram 35**), taking care not to stretch the bias. With right sides facing, align the raw edges (indicated as Seam 2). As you align the edges, offset one Seam 2 point past its natural matching point by one line. Stitch the seam; then press the seam allowance open.

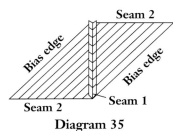

Diagram 35

3. Cut the binding in a continuous strip, starting with the protruding point and following the marked lines around the tube (**Diagram 36**). Press the strip in half lengthwise.

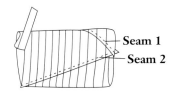

Diagram 36

Applying Binding

Binding is applied to the front of the quilt first. You may begin anywhere on the edge of the quilt except at the corner.

1. Matching raw edges, lay the binding on the quilt. Fold down the top corner of the binding at a 45° angle, align the raw edges, and pin (**Diagram 37**).

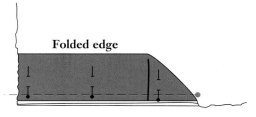

Folded edge

Diagram 37

2. Beginning at the folded end, machine-stitch the binding to the quilt. Stop stitching ¼" from the corner and backstitch. Fold the binding strip diagonally away from the quilt, making a 45° angle (**Diagram 38**).

3. Fold the binding strip straight down along the next side to be stitched, creating a pleat in the corner. Position the needle at the ¼" seam line of the new side (**Diagram 39**). Make a few stitches, backstitch, and then stitch the seam. Continue until all corners and sides are done. Overlap the end of the binding strip over the beginning fold and stitch about 2" beyond it. Trim any excess binding.

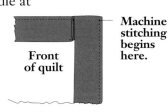

Front of quilt

Diagram 38

Machine stitching begins here.

Front of quilt

Diagram 39

4. Turn the binding over the raw edge of the quilt. Slipstitch it in place on the back, using thread that matches the binding. The fold at the beginning of the binding strip will create a neat, angled edge when it is folded to the back.

5. At each corner, fold the binding to form a miter (**Diagram 40**). Hand-stitch the miters closed if desired.

Back of quilt

Diagram 40

Quilt by Susan Stein
Saint Paul, Minnesota

Amish Friendship Sampler

The following pages contain directions and patterns to stitch, block by block, this beautiful quilt designed and made by award-winning quilter Susan Stein. Below you'll find fabric requirements for reproducing Susan's scrap quilt. Or feel free to pick a color scheme of your own, letting your own scrap bag be your guide.

We've given you cutting instructions and piecing diagrams with each block illustration. We've also included special piecing and quick-cutting information where appropriate. Instructions for completing your quilt are on page 40, and a complete set of template patterns begins on page 42.

Finished Quilt Size
87" x 95"

Number of Blocks and Finished Size
12 sampler blocks	12" x 12"
112 Flying Geese blocks	3⅛" x 6¼"
56 Pinwheel blocks	6¼" x 6¼"

Fabric Requirements
Dark green	¼ yard
Light green	¼ yard or fat ⅛
Light blue	⅝ yard
Medium blue	¼ yard or fat ⅛
Dark blue	¼ yard or fat ⅛
Aqua	⅛ yard
Fuchsia	¼ yard
Lavender	⅜ yard
Purple	¼ yard or fat ⅛
Dark purple	¼ yard or fat ⅛
Pink	¼ yard or fat ⅛
Light pink	¼ yard
Teal	⅛ yard
Maroon	¼ yard
Rust	⅜ yard or fat ¼
Tan	⅜ yard
Brown	¼ yard
Mauve	¼ yard
Muslin	½ yard
Black	2½ yards
Black for binding	1 yard
Backing	8 yards
Pinwheels	1½ yards total assorted scraps or 112 (4") squares
Flying Geese	3¼ yards total assorted scraps or 112 (3⅝") squares and 112 (6¾" x 3⅝") rectangles

Weathervane

Susan's friends signed each sampler block in this quilt,
making it an extra-special friendship quilt.

Number to Cut

(Template patterns begin on page 42.)

Template A   1 muslin

Template B   4 dark green

Template C   8 mauve
                   16 light blue

Template D   4 mauve
                   4 light blue

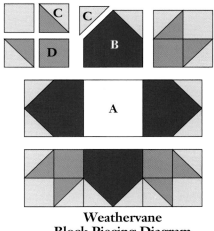

**Weathervane
Block Piecing Diagram**

Original Color

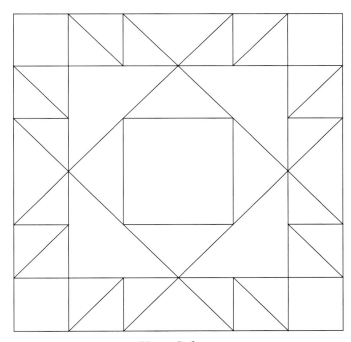

Your Color

Quick Tip

See page 39 for a quick way to piece half-square triangles for this block.

Stepping Stones

The four corners of this block are actually simple nine-patches. Before you begin, read "Quick-pieced Nine-Patch" on the facing page.

Number to Cut

(Template patterns begin on page 42.)

Template E   1 tan

Template F   20 light green
                       16 light blue

Template G   8 tan

Template H   8 rust

Template I   4 light blue

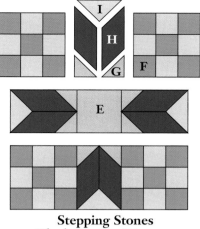

**Stepping Stones
Block Piecing Diagram**

Original Color

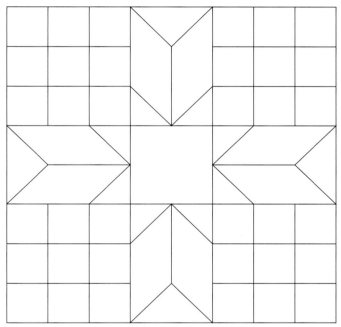

Your Color

Quick-pieced Nine-Patch

Nine-patches are easy to make using strip-piecing. To strip piece the four nine-patches in this block, cut 2 (2½" x 30") strips from light green and 1 (2½" x 40") strip from light blue. Cut each green strip into 1 (20") length and 1 (10") length. Cut blue strip into 1 (20") length and 2 (10") lengths.

Join 1 (20") green strip to each side of 20" blue strip as shown in **Figure A** to make a pieced band. Repeat procedure with remaining 10" strips, alternating colors. Referring to **Figure B** and using your rotary cutter and ruler, cut across the seams of each band at 2½" intervals to form 8 green/blue/green units and 4 blue/green/blue units. Join units as shown in Block Piecing Diagram to form four nine-patch blocks.

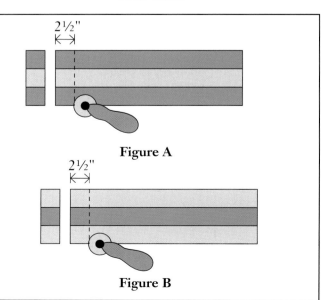

2½"

Figure A

2½"

Figure B

Rising Sun

You can make this block with the template patterns in the back of the book. Or take a shortcut and make the eight Flying Geese units following the directions on page 38.

Number to Cut

(Template patterns begin on page 42.)

Template E	1 aqua
	4 lavender
Template F	4 muslin
Template G	8 teal
Template I	4 muslin
Template J	4 lavender
Template K	8 purple

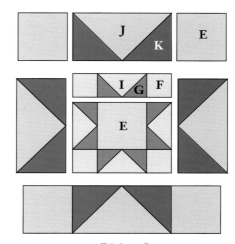

Rising Sun
Block Piecing Diagram

Original Color

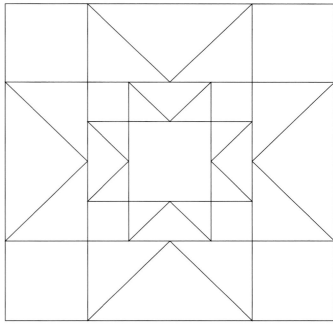

Your Color

Five-Patch Star

This block requires sewing set-in seams. Before you
begin, read "Easy Set-in Seams" on page 23.

Number to Cut

(Template patterns begin on page 42.)

Template L	1 light pink
Template M	4 light green
Template N	4 mauve
Template O	4 light blue
Template O rev.	4 light blue
Template P	8 dark green 4 light blue

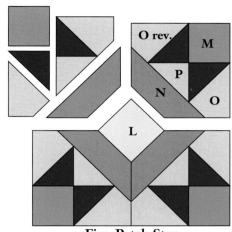

Five-Patch Star
Block Piecing Diagram

Original Color

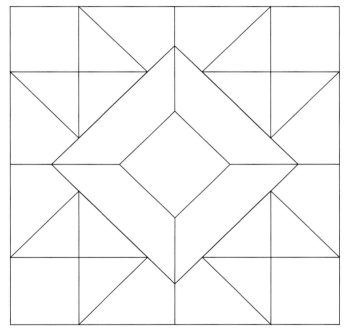

Your Color

Many-Pointed Star

Sewing set-in seams isn't hard if you follow the directions on the facing page.

Number to Cut

(Template patterns begin on page 42.)

Template E   4 muslin

Template H   4 pink
                           4 fuchsia
                           8 brown

Template I   8 muslin

Template Q   1 light pink

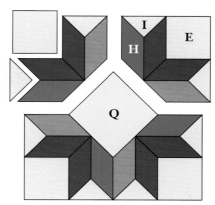

**Many-Pointed Star
Block Piecing Diagram**

Original Color

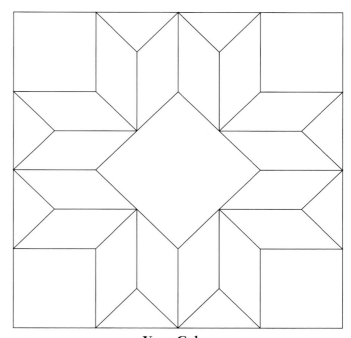

Your Color

Easy Set-In Seams

When piecing diamonds or other angled seams, you may need to make set-in seams. For these, always mark the corner dots of the seam allowances (shown on the patterns) on the fabric pieces. Stitch one side, starting at the outside edge and being careful not to sew beyond the dot into the seam allowance **(Figure A).** Backstitch. Align the other side of the piece as needed, with right sides facing. Sew from the dot to the outside edge **(Figure B).**

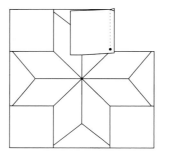

Figure A

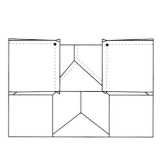

Figure B

Puss in the Corner

The four corners of this block look like a traditional nine-patch at first, but the center of each checkerboard is a different color.

Number to Cut

(Template patterns begin on page 42.)

Template R   16 dark blue
                     4 muslin
                16 light blue

Template S   4 light pink

Template T   4 mauve

Template GG   1 muslin

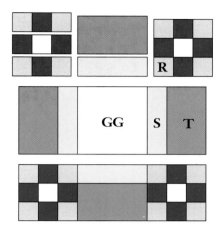

**Puss in the Corner
Block Piecing Diagram**

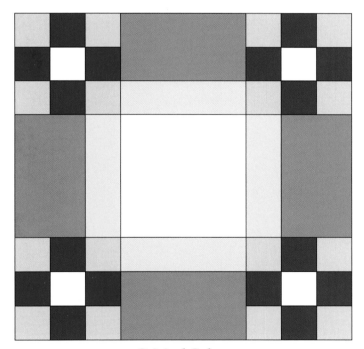

Original Color

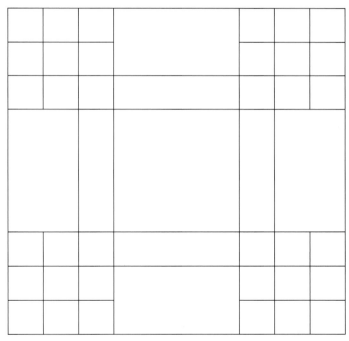

Your Color

Lotus Star

Be sure to cut your pieces carefully from the templates in the back of this book. Some of these triangles are unusual sizes!

Number to Cut

(Template patterns begin on page 42.)

Template D   8 lavender

Template I   8 lavender

Template U   1 light blue

Template V   16 fuchsia

Template W   4 aqua

Template W rev.   4 aqua

Template X   4 teal

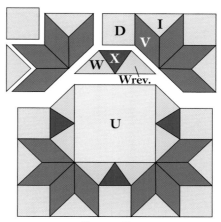

Lotus Star
Block Piecing Diagram

Original Color

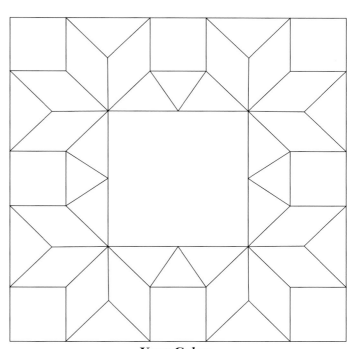

Your Color

Quick Tip

See page 23 for information on sewing set-in seams.

Album

This block has unusually sized pieces, so use the templates in the back of this book and cut carefully.

Number to Cut

(Template patterns begin on page 42.)

Template Y   4 rust
                   4 maroon
                   8 tan
                  16 muslin

Template Z   4 rust
                   8 maroon
                   4 muslin

Template AA   1 lavender

Template BB   2 lavender

**Album
Block Piecing Diagram**

Original Color

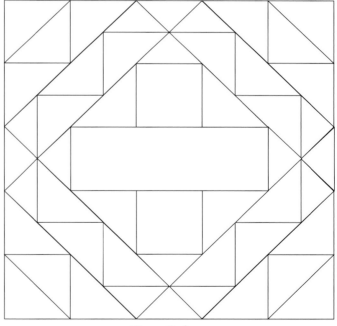

Your Color

Union Square Variation

Read "Cutting Triangles from Squares" on the facing
page before beginning this block. You can also use the
quick-piecing methods on pages 38 and 39.

Number to Cut

(Template patterns begin on page 42.)

Template A	1 lavender
Template C	16 dark green 8 light blue
Template D	4 light blue
Template CC	4 light blue 4 rust
Template DD	4 tan

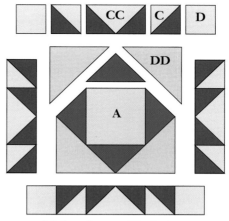

**Union Square Variation
Block Piecing Diagram**

Original Color

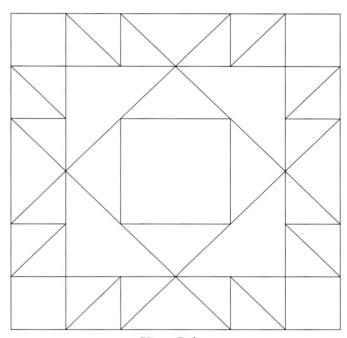

Your Color

Cutting Triangles from Squares

To cut *half-square triangles* from squares, measure the finished size of the leg or short side of the triangle and add ⅞" to this number. Cut a strip of fabric this width and cut the squares from this strip. Cut the square in half diagonally to form half-square triangles.

Short side (leg) + ⅞"

Half-square triangles

To cut *quarter-square triangles* from squares, measure the finished size of the longest side or hypotenuse of the triangle. To that measurement, add 1¼" and cut a strip of fabric that width. Cut a square from that strip, then cut the square in half diagonally in both directions.

Longest side (hypotenuse) + 1¼"

Quarter-square triangles

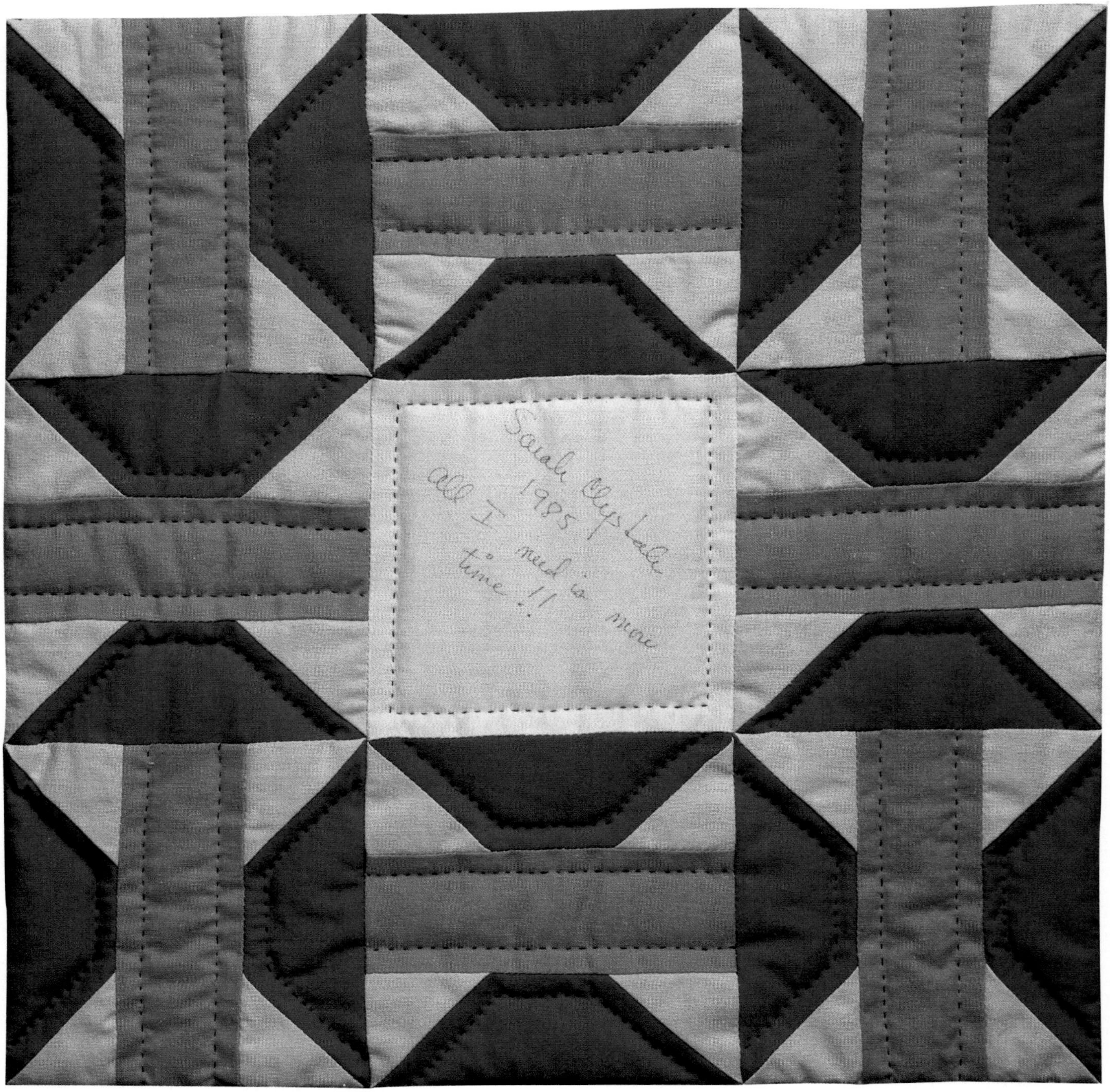
1985
All I need is more
time!!

Beggar's Block

Turn each patch in this block so that the center stripes are perpendicular to each other.

Number to Cut

(Template patterns begin on page 42.)

Template A   1 light blue

Template EE   16 blue

Template FF   32 tan

Template HH   8 brown

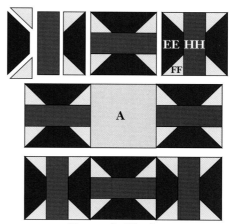

Beggar's Block
Block Piecing Diagram

Original Color

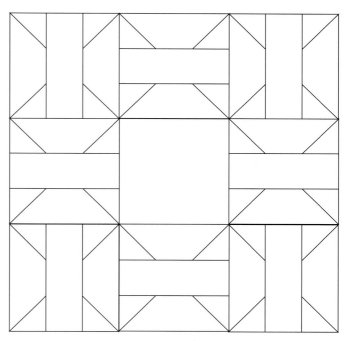

Your Color

Single Irish Chain

Before you begin this block, read "Quick-pieced Four-Patch" on the facing page.

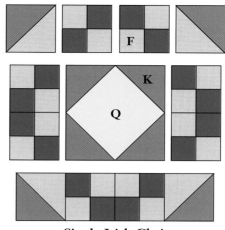

Number to Cut

(Template patterns begin on page 42.)

Template F   16 rust
                 16 tan

Template K   8 medium blue
                 4 tan

Template Q   1 light pink

**Single Irish Chain
Block Piecing Diagram**

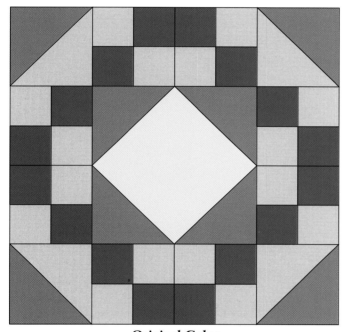

Original Color

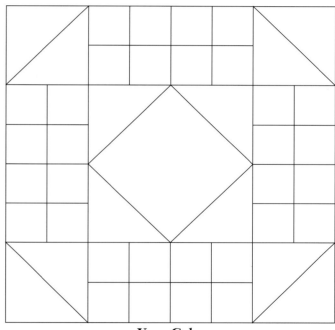

Your Color

Quick-pieced Four-Patch

Four-patches are easy to make using strip-piecing. To strip-piece the eight four-patches in this block, cut 1 (2" x 32") strip each from light gray and rust. Join strips along one long edge to make a pieced band. Using your rotary cutter and ruler, cut across the seam of this band at 2" intervals to form 16 units. (See diagram at right.) Join units as shown in **Block Piecing Diagram** to form eight four-patch blocks.

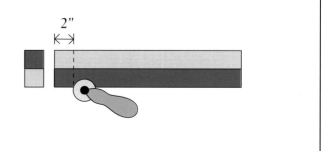

Quick Tip

See page 39 for a quick way to piece half-square triangles for this block.

Jefferson City

For easier cutting, read "Cutting Triangles from Squares" on the page 31 before beginning this block.

Number to Cut

(Template patterns begin on page 42.)

Template A   1 light blue

Template L   4 lavender
               4 purple

Template CC   4 medium blue
              12 muslin

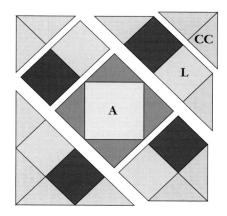

Jefferson City
Block Piecing Diagram

Original Color

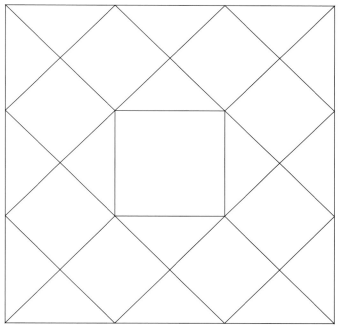

Original Color

Flying Geese

Susan mixed a few color "mistakes" into her Flying Geese according to Amish tradition. She thinks perfect color placement can be boring, so Susan suggests you add a few mistakes of your own!

Number to Cut

(Use templates beginning on page 42 or the method described below.)

Template II   112
Template JJ   224

**Flying Geese
Block Piecing Diagram**

Diagonal-Corners Method for Flying Geese

This method for making Flying Geese blocks eliminates cutting triangles.

To determine the size of the squares and rectangles to cut for your blocks, you must first know your finished block size. (You'll find that information with quilt directions.) The width of a traditional Flying Geese block is twice its height. That is, if the block is 3" high, it should be 6" wide. For this quilt, each block is 3⅛" x 6¼".

For each Flying Geese block, you will cut 2 squares equal to the block's finished height, plus ¼" on each side for seam allowance; and you will cut 1 rectangle equal to the size of the finished block plus ¼" on each side for seam allowance. For example: For the finished 3⅛" x 6¼" block in this quilt, you will cut 2 (3⅝") squares and 1 (3⅝" x 6¾") rectangle.

Follow these steps to quick-piece flying geese the diagonal corners way:

1. Fold each square in half diagonally and crease or press fold. Or lightly draw a line from one corner to the other.

2. With right sides facing, place one square on one rectangle as shown in **Figure A.** Using the creased or drawn line as a stitching line, stitch through both layers from one corner of the square to the other as shown. It is crucial that you stitch a straight line from point to point.

3. Using your rotary cutter, trim the corner of your block, leaving ¼" seam allowance as shown in **Figure B.**

4. Press seam toward triangle corner.

5. Place another square (with diagonal drawn or creased) on top of this unit as shown in **Figure C.** Stitch across it diagonally.

6. Trim corner, leaving ¼" seam allowance as shown in **Figure D.**

7. Press seam toward corner. **Figure E** shows finished block.

Figure A

Figure B

Figure C

Figure D

Figure E

Pinwheels

Twenty-eight Pinwheels may seem daunting at first, but you'll be surprised how quickly they come together with the quick-piecing technique described on this page.

Number to Cut
(Use templates beginning on page 42 or the method described below.)

Template JJ   224

**Pinwheels
Block Piecing Diagram**

Making Triangle Squares

When two same-size right triangles are joined along diagonal edges to form a square, it is called a triangle square. Each triangle equals half the square.

1. The project instructions illustrate and describe the grid, stating the number and size of the squares needed. These squares are 7/8" larger on each side than the leg (short side) of the desired finished triangle. Draw diagonal lines through the grid as illustrated **(Figure A).**

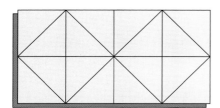

Figure A

2. Match the marked fabric to its companion fabric, with right sides facing. Pin the layers together along horizontal and vertical lines, avoiding diagonal lines so the pins will not interfere with stitching.

3. Machine-stitch 1/4" from both sides of all diagonal lines **(Figure B).** At corners, pivot the fabric without lifting the needle.

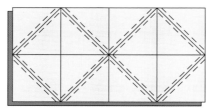

Figure B

4. When stitching is done, trim the excess fabric around the grid; then cut on all horizontal and vertical drawn lines, cutting the fabric into squares **(Figure C).**

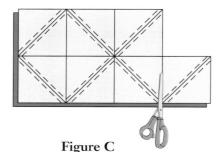

Figure C

5. Next, cut on the diagonal drawn line between the stitching **(Figure D).**

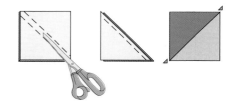

Figure D

6. Press seam allowances toward the darker fabric. Cut points off the seam allowances, making a neat square. Be careful not to pull on the seam, as this will stretch the bias and distort the square.

Sashing and Borders

Number to Cut

3½" x 12½"	10 black
3½" x 87½"	6 black
4½" x 87½"	2 black
4½" x 88"	2 black

Quilt Top Assembly

1. Referring to **Assembly Diagram,** alternate 5 (3½" x 12½") sashing strips with 6 sampler blocks. Join to form 1 sampler block row. Repeat with remaining 5 sashing strips and 6 sampler blocks.

2. Join 28 Flying Geese blocks to form 1 Flying Geese row. Repeat to form 4 Flying Geese rows.

3. Join 14 Pinwheel blocks to form 1 Pinwheel row. Repeat to form 2 Pinwheel rows. Join 2 Pinwheel rows together to form 1 Pinwheel section.

4. Referring to **Assembly Diagram,** alternate 3½" x 87½" sashing strips with Flying Geese rows, sampler block rows, and Pinwheel section, and join.

5. Join side borders to quilt top, then join top and bottom borders to quilt top.

Quilting

Quilt as desired.

Finishing

Referring to instructions on page 11, make 10¼ yards of 2"-wide bias or straight-grain binding from black. Apply binding to edges of quilt.

Quilt Top Assembly Diagram

Template Patterns

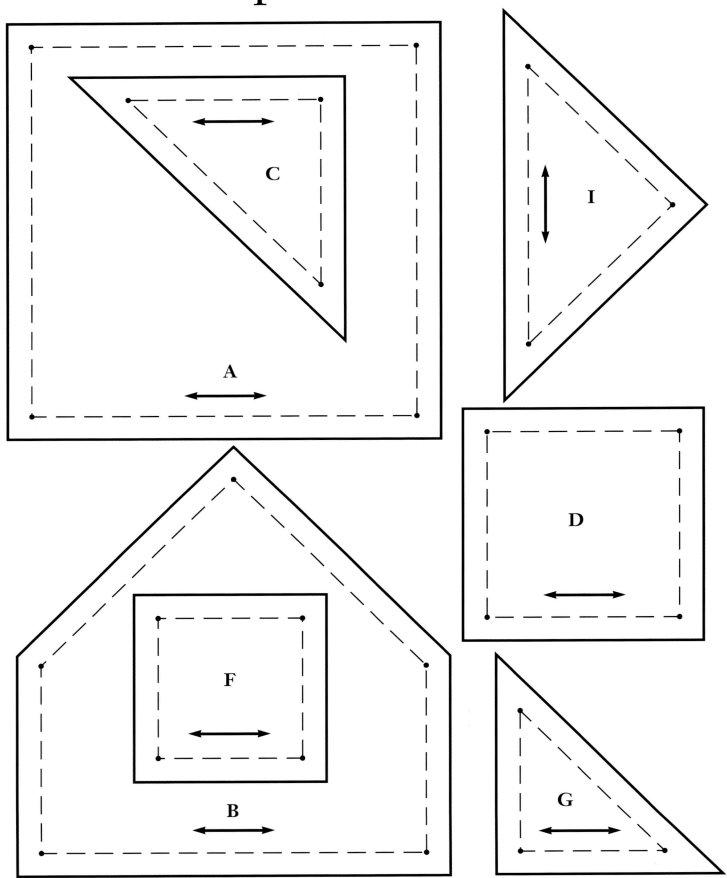

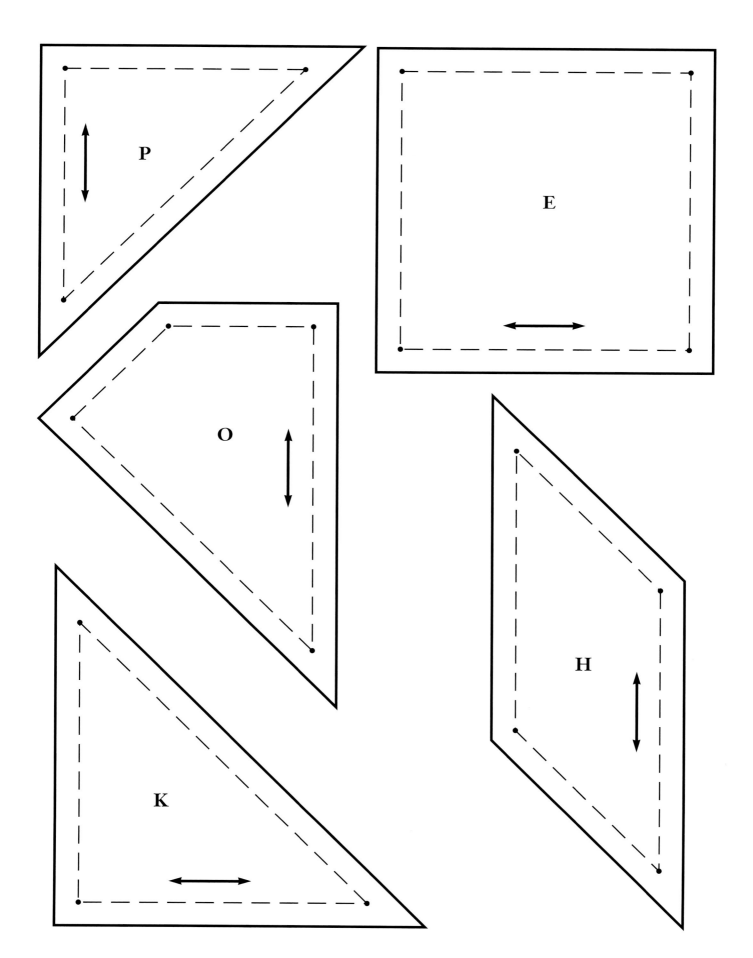

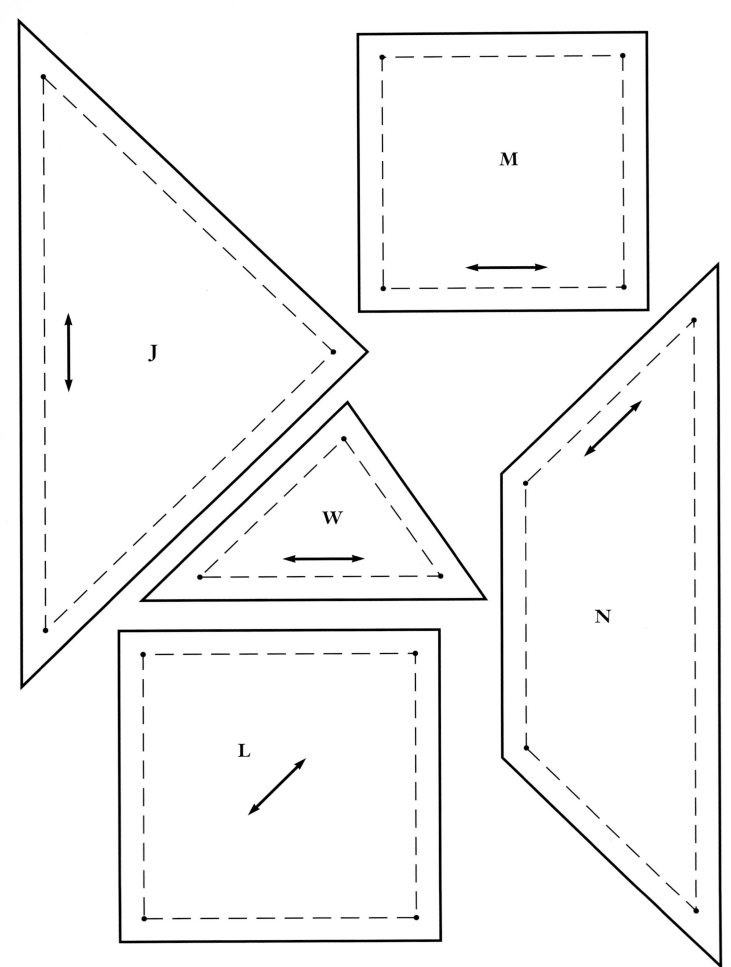

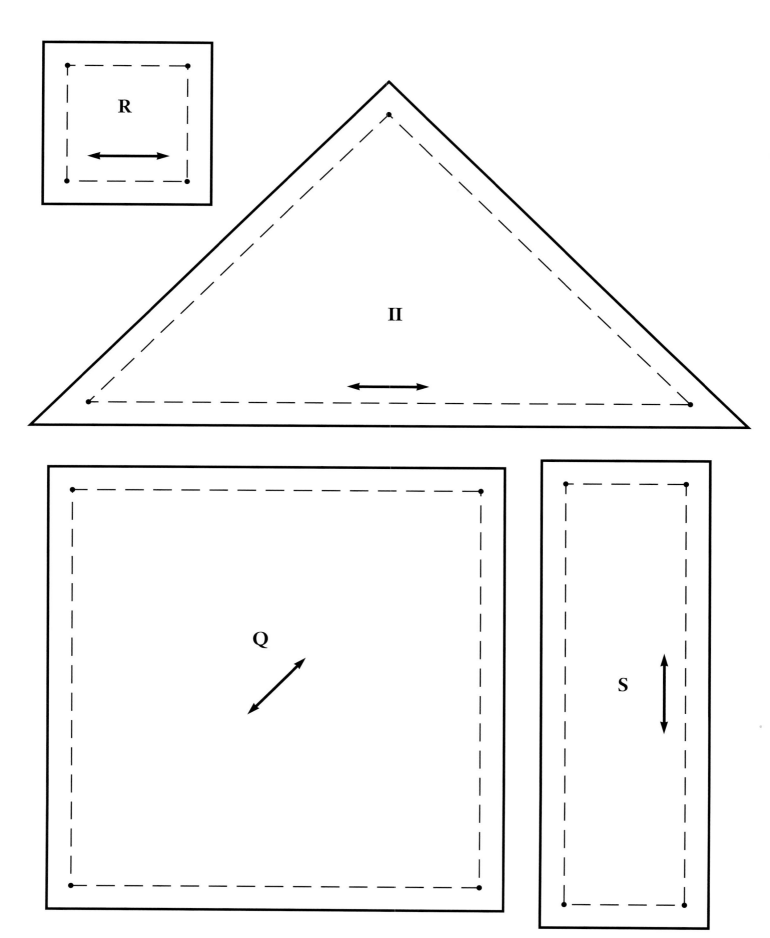

R

II

Q

S

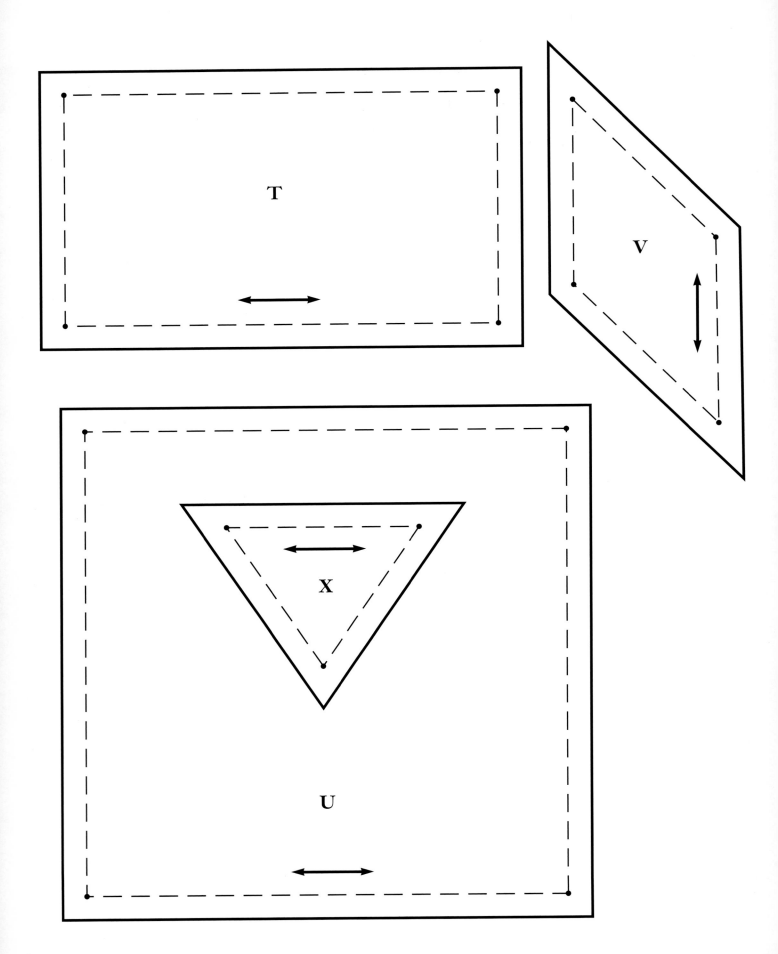

T

V

X

U

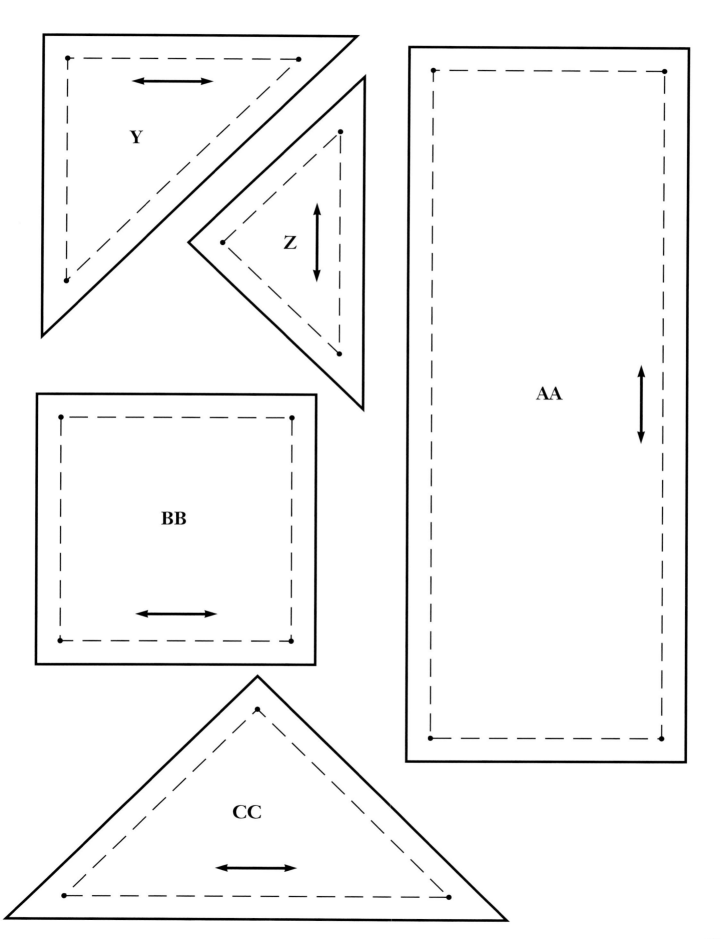

Y

Z

AA

BB

CC

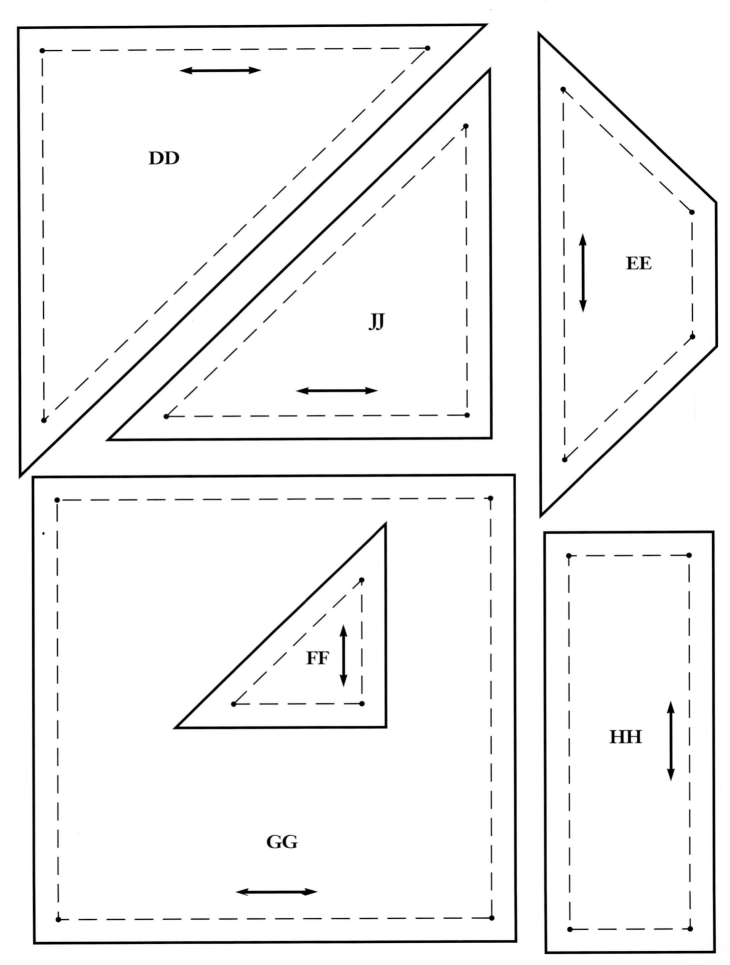

DD

JJ

EE

FF

GG

HH

48